Ancient City of the Inca

by Michael Sandler

SCHOOL PUBLISHERS

Printed in the United States of America

ISBN 10: 0-15-351704-2
ISBN 13: 978-0-15-351704-4

Ordering Options
ISBN 10: 0-15-351704-2 (Grade 6 Advanced Collection)
ISBN 13: 978-0-15-351704-4 (Grade 6 Advanced Collection)
ISBN 10: 0-15-358187-5 (package of 5)
ISBN 13: 978-0-15-358187-8 (package of 5)

2 3 4 5 6 7 8 9 10   179   12 11 10 09 08 07

It stood alone in the jungle for centuries, hidden high in the mountains. It was safe from trespassers. No one would stumble across this place. Covered in vines and trees, the city was slowly decaying. Only a few knew about it. Then, after a prolonged period of isolation, the lost city was rediscovered.

The place was Peru, a country that lies along the west coast of South America. The year was 1911. An explorer named Hiram Bingham was on an expedition. He was searching for an ancient city. He wanted to find the place called Vitcos. This was the last battleground of the Inca, once the mightiest people in the Americas.

The Inca

Little is known about the earliest history of the Inca. They had no written language, so no written record of their origin exists. They did have legends that were passed down through oral tradition. According to one tale, the Inca began with eight people. They founded a town called Cuzco in the Andes. The Andes is the greatest mountain range in South America. It stretches north and south for the length of the continent. There one of the eight, Manco Capac, became the very first Inca king.

3

Eventually, the Inca became a powerful force. They conquered other groups of people and increased their territory. Eventually the Inca Empire covered thousands of square miles. In time, much of South America fell under the power of one Inca ruler. By the late fifteenth century, the Inca Empire included parts of six present-day countries. The Inca called their empire the "land of the four quarters." At its heart was the capital in Cuzco. From here, the empire stretched out in four directions. It stretched north along the mountains. It stretched south toward present-day Chile. It went west to the Pacific Ocean. It went east across the Amazon rain forest.

The empire was divided into small provinces. Each province had its own leader. This leader was loyal to the Inca king. Holding everything together were miles and miles of roads. Provinces were strategically linked by a huge transportation network. In all, there were nearly 15,000 miles (24,140 km) of roads. Two main highways followed the line of the Andes. Smaller roads joined these highways from the east and west.

As many as ten million people lived under Inca rule. Many spoke a form of Quechua, a language still used today. Most were farmers. Many farmed on terraces because it was difficult to farm the mountainous land. To do so, they cut flat fields into the mountainsides. Potatoes were the most important crop. Farmers grew hundreds of different kinds. A portion of everything grown went to the rulers. Labor had to be delivered as well. When called, subjects had to help construct roads and temples or serve in the empire's army.

While life for the average person was hard, Inca rulers lived in luxury. In Cuzco, they inhabited palaces. They walked through gardens filled with lustrous plants. The plants weren't real. Instead, they were formed from gold.

Fall of the Empire

The empire reached its peak in the early sixteenth century. Then it was torn apart. Civil war played a role. Two brothers battled for control of the kingdom. The conflict happened at a very unlucky time. Just when the Inca needed strength, they were weak. European invaders were about to arrive.

In 1532, Spanish conquistadors (soldier-explorers) arrived in the Inca Empire. They were led by a man named Francisco Pizarro. Pizarro had heard about the Inca Empire. He was hungry for Inca gold. Pizarro's force was tiny. With him were fewer than two hundred men. Still, that number turned out to be more than enough. In the town of Cajamarca, Pizarro's forces captured the Incan emperor, Atahualpa. They promised to release him in exchange for a huge ransom in gold. The Incans complied.

Soon massive amounts of gold were delivered to the Spaniards. It was enough to fill an entire room. Today such an amount would be worth more than fifty million dollars. After the gold arrived, however, Pizarro broke his promise. Atahualpa wasn't released. Instead the emperor was killed. The Spanish forces continued on. They marched 700 miles (1,127 km) to Cuzco and took over the capital.

By the late 1500s, the Inca were completely defeated. Their empire had fallen apart. Their land was claimed by Spain and would be ruled by Spain for centuries. The Incan gold work was melted down into coins and bars. Inca temples were torn down and replaced by Spanish churches. Many Incan towns were destroyed or abandoned. Many Inca died. Some had fallen to Spanish swords. Many more were killed by disease. European diseases like smallpox killed millions in the Americas. The Native Americans had no resistance to them.

Descendants of the Inca still live in Peru and neighboring countries today. Many speak Quechua and other languages of the Inca Empire.

The Explorer

Hiram Bingham was a professor at Yale University. An archaeologist, he had long been interested in the Inca. He had read about their history. He had studied their legends. Several journeys to South America preceded his 1911 trip.

On this journey, Bingham was looking for Vitcos. This was the city the last Incan rulers fled. Here the final battle with the Spanish took place. After the Spanish won, the city was burned. The ruins were swallowed by the jungle. Bingham was focused on finding these ruins. He knew it wouldn't be easy. He was resigned to a long journey.

Bingham began his trip in Lima, Peru's capital. From there, he went to Cuzco and headed north. Bingham's party followed an old path into an ancient river valley. A week into the trip, while camped on the river's banks, he met a local farmer, who told Bingham about some ruins across the river. They were located by a mountain called Machu Picchu. Bingham asked the farmer to guide him there. At first, the farmer refused. The trip was too difficult, he said. Then Bingham offered to pay him. The farmer's temperament changed. He agreed to make the trip.

The journey was both difficult and frightening. The route led through dense patches of jungle. The guide warned of poisonous snakes. Bingham did as he was told. He and his guide crawled across rickety bridges. They scrambled up steep cliffs. On and on they walked, fighting the heat and humidity.

Finally, they arrived. The spot was almost in the clouds, tucked away between two towering peaks. It was a maze of stonework, the remains of an ancient city. Most was overgrown with vines, bushes, trees, and moss. As Bingham walked around, he saw walls, streets, and temples. This was the finest Incan stonework Bingham had ever seen.

"I could scarcely believe my senses," wrote Bingham later. "Would anyone believe what I had found?"

The City

Bingham made several trips to this place called Machu Picchu. He brought teams of scientists to map and study the ruins. They took thousands of photographs. They dug for Incan artifacts, collecting thousands. They searched for the answers to many questions. What was the place used for? When was it built? Why was it abandoned? Why had it been hidden so long?

Over the years, many of these questions have been answered. The place was almost certainly picked for its remoteness. High in the mountains, nearly 8,000 feet (2,438 m) above sea level, Machu Picchu was safe from enemy attack. No one would accidentally find it.

The city is around four hundred years old. Though Bingham thought he'd found Vitcos, he was mistaken. Five decades later, other ruins were found that are thought to be the place of the last stand of the Inca. Not only was it not Vitcos, Machu Picchu wasn't a normal city at all. Judging by the buildings and layout, some believe the place was a royal retreat. When Incan nobles and their families needed a vacation, this was where they went.

The abandonment of Machu Picchu remains a mystery. It wasn't the Spanish invasion that caused it. The Spanish never reached Machu Picchu. Perhaps the city was struck by disease. Perhaps a rival group of people attacked. There are many different theories. No one really knows the answer. How the city was built remains something of a mystery, too. The Inca never used the wheel. To get building materials to and around the site must have taken the labor of thousands.

There is no question, however, about the talents of its builders. Machu Picchu has several different levels. They are linked by stone staircases—over a hundred in all. Some are carved from a single huge piece of stone.

A system of aqueducts, or water channels, runs through the site. These provided water for fields, fountains, and royal baths. There are temples, tombs, palaces, and structures for storing grain. All are built from stone, cut into neatly shaped blocks. The Inca had no iron tools to cut stone. They used no mortar to bind walls. Still, the blocks fit together like puzzle pieces. Even today, after hundreds of years, the fit is astoundingly tight. A knife blade can't pass between them.

Windows and doors share a unique shape. They are wide at the bottom. Toward the top they narrow. The shape wasn't chosen for beauty. The design makes the buildings stronger. It helps them to withstand the earthquakes that are common in Peru.

Machu Picchu Today

Today Machu Picchu is one of the greatest historic attractions in South America. The ancient city draws tourists from across the world. Every year, about half a million people head here. Unlike Hiram Bingham, they don't have to wade through the jungle to find the ruins. Getting there is much easier than it was in 1911.

International plane flights bring visitors right into Cuzco. Then it's off to Aguas Calientes, a pleasant four-hour ride from Cuzco by train. The most luxurious train service features live music and a four-course meal. The train is named the "Hiram Bingham." From Aguas Calientes, it's just a fifteen-minute bus ride up to the gates of the ancient city.

Some tourists choose to get to Machu Picchu the old-fashioned way. They walk. Hiking the Inca trail is a four-day trip. Travelers stroll along stone footpaths built by the Incan rulers. Along the way, they stop and camp. Even this mode of transportation isn't very difficult. Porters carry all the equipment—tents, sleeping bags, and supplies. Travelers just need to walk and admire the breathtaking Andean scenery.

In the future, however, visiting Machu Picchu may become more difficult. Officials worry about the parade of visitors. They worry about the damage it is causing to the historic spot. Each day, thousands of pounding feet tear up the grass and wear down stone pathways. Tour buses pour into the parking lot spewing smoke into the mountain air.

In response to these problems, Peru has announced plans to limit the number of visitors. Only a certain number will be allowed into Machu Picchu each day. Already, the number of trekkers on the Inca Trail is limited. To get one of 500 daily permits, visitors must plan far in advance.

Still, it will be hard to cut tourism too much. People will always want to see these unique ruins. Also, tourism brings badly needed income. Local people depend on tourism-related jobs. Many work in nearby restaurants and hotels, or earn their livings as drivers, guides, and porters.

One tour operator says, "No one wants to see Machu Picchu damaged . . . but no one wants to lose their livelihoods either."

The Case of Bingham's Artifacts

Another controversy involving Machu Picchu has to do with the work of Hiram Bingham. The explorer made trips to Machu Picchu in 1911, 1912, and 1915. Each time he came home, he brought crates of objects with him. These were Incan relics and artifacts found at Machu Picchu. The objects varied. They included bones, pots, and tools. All had once been part of the Incan city.

The objects ended up in Connecticut, at a Yale University museum. Officials in Peru took notice. They said the objects belonged to Peru, not Yale. They were loaned, not given, to the university.

Like any other borrowed objects, says Peru, these artifacts must be restored to their rightful owners. The objects were found in Peru, they say, so they belong to Peru. The university has been asked to return them. Yale, however, disagrees. The school says that it owns the objects—though it has offered to return part of the collection. The exact number of artifacts and relics is also a point of disagreement. Peru says there are 5,000. Yale says there are many fewer.

Peru and Yale are in talks about the issue. Hopefully, they will find a way to settle the problem by 2011. That year will be the hundredth anniversary of Machu Picchu's rediscovery by Bingham.

Yale University

Think Critically

1. What was Hiram Bingham looking for when he found Machu Picchu?

2. Why did the Spanish arrive at a very bad time for the Inca?

3. Do you think tourism should be limited at Machu Picchu? Why or why not?

4. What are Yale University and Peru doing to try and resolve the problem of the Incan artifacts?

5. Compare and contrast how Machu Picchu today is different from when Bingham first saw it in 1911.

 Social Studies

Historic Sites Brainstorm three ancient cities or other historic sites you'd like to visit. Do some research on these places and write a paragraph on each, explaining why you'd like to travel to these places.

 School-Home Connection Share what you learned about Machu Picchu with a friend or family member. Talk about what you found most interesting about what you read about Machu Picchu.

Word Count: 2,159 (with graphic 2,168)